Flags

Boris Poplavsky

FLAGS

translated by
Belinda Cooke & Richard McKane

Shearsman Books
Exeter

First published in in the United Kingdom in 2009 by
Shearsman Books Ltd
58 Velwell Road
Exeter EX4 4LD

www.shearsman.com

ISBN 978-1-84861-060-6
First Edition

Translations copyright © Belinda Cooke and Richard McKane, 2009.

The right of Belinda Cooke and Richard McKane to be identified
as the translators of this work has been asserted by them in accordance
with the Copyrights, Designs and Patents Act of 1988.
All rights reserved.

Acknowledgements

The translators are particularly indebted to Peter Jay of Anvil Press Poetry for permission to include translations from the anthology, *Surviving the Twentieth Century: Ten Russian Poets*, (Anvil Press Poetry, 2002). Some of the translations have appeared in the following publications to whose editors grateful thanks are offered: *Acumen, Agenda, Gnosis, Modern Poetry in Translation, Poetry Salzburg Review, Shearsman, Stand, Tears in the Fence* and *Washington House*.

We owe special thanks to Olga Sevastyanova who gave up hours of her time checking the Russian of the text.

Hélène Menagaldo and Leonid Livak's years of research into Poplavsky were invaluable in introducing us to the poet. Their work and other useful books are listed in the bibliography. We also drew heavily on Boris Poplavsky's *Sochinenia* (Collected Works, 1999), ed. S.A. Ivanova, to assist us with the translations.

Finally, we will be ever grateful to the people who first introduced us separately to Boris Poplavsky's work. In the case of Richard this was Victoria Andreyeva, and for Belinda, the Russian émigré writer Olga Andreyev Carlisle who dedicated most of her life to increasing knowledge of Russian poets in the West and who, as a Russian émigré herself, knew Poplavsky personally as well as many other émigré poets when she was growing up.

Contents

Introduction   9

Flags

Eagles   17
Transformation into Stone   18
'How cold the public waters are'   19
Disgust   20
In a Garland of Wax   21
Immobility   22
The Magic Lantern   23
Joint Reign   24
An Attempt with Inadequate Means   25
In a Struggle with the Snow   26
Army Stanzas   27
Rain   28
Sentimental Demonology   29
The Angels of Hell   31
A Struggle with Sleep   32
An Imitation to Zhukovsky   33
Spring in Hell   34
Don Quixote   35
'The negative pole is silent and shines'   37
Astral World   38
Paysage d'enfer   40
A Starlit Hell   41
To Arthur Rimbaud   42
The Black Madonna   44
Diabolique   46
The Last Parade   48
At Dawn   50
Mercy   51
'The rose-coloured hour floated over the dawning world'   52
Dolorosa   53
The Rose of Death   54
'The delightful evening is full of smiles and sounds'   55
The Moonlit Airship   56

Manuscript Found in a Bottle	58
Hamlet	60
Flags	61
Mystic Rondo I	62
Roman Morning	63
Mystic Rondo II	64
The Goddess of Life	65
The Death of the Children	67
Hamlet's Childhood	68
'The little girl returned, the angel began to sing at random'	69
The Black Hare	70
Homage to Pablo Picasso	72
The Boy and the Angel	74
Pentecost	75
Under the Earth	76
Stars' Poison	77
Salome I	78
Salome II	80
Roses of the Grail	82
The Passing	83
Pity for Europe	84
The Spirit of Music	86
Angélique	87
In the Distance	89
Winter	90
Remember—Resurrect	91
Death Island	92
Air Spirit	93
Lumière astrale	94
Mystic Rondo III	95
Morella I	97
Morella II	98
Seraphita I	99
Seraphita II	100
Stoicism	101
'The whole day in a cold, dirty shroud'	103
'The world was dark, cold transparent'	104
'The sun sinks, it's still so hot'	105

Supplementary to *Flags*

'Each cold soul burns with dawn's light'	109
'Ancient history is full of blue and pink stars'	110
'My moon I can dream about you again'	111
'The pale blue soul of the ray'	113
'The boy is looking, the white boat'	114
'Autumn walks beyond the walls of life'	116
'The supernatural knight on a horse'	117
'The air is dark. In the sky roses are soaring'	119
'Night revolved around the trumpet of the orchestra'	121
Bibliography	122

In memoriam Victoria Andreyeva
who loved Poplavsky's poetry

and

for Olga Andreyev Carlisle

Introduction

Boris Poplavsky: The Hamlet of Montparnasse

Boris Poplavsky is a well-kept Russian secret. Little known even to Russian residents until the relaxations of *Glasnost'* in 1989 his life is as intriguing as his strange dreamlike, often mystifying poems. Why he has lain so long undiscovered outside a very small group of academics is part of just one more chapter in Russia's tragic waves of emigration—the lost generation neither famous at home or abroad struggling to gain recognition in their new home. Poplavsky was just one of the thousands of Russians fleeing the Civil War to arrive, and have to adapt from a life of relative comfort to a struggle to survive, along with the psychological disorientation of émigré life. Yet, complexes in Poplavsky's self and family background suggest he would always have been a tortured soul and his particular émigré situation only exacerbated a difficult emotional makeup.

Poplavsky was born in June 1903 to two very different parents: his father was a Polish peasant while his mother, who came from a landed Baltic background, suffered attacks of depression as well as a fascination with mysticism. She was associated with Madame Blavatsky and her circle. Although Poplavsky had a healthy relationship with his father, that with his mother was troubled and contributed to bouts of mental illness throughout his life. His upbringing was not one that he remembered with much pleasure, describing its atmosphere as prison-like. In addition, during his childhood, his ties with the Russian language were disrupted by his younger sister's tuberculosis which forced the family to spend extensive periods in Switzerland and Italy; Poplavsky's Russian deteriorated so much that he had to be enrolled in a French lycée after his return to Moscow. Another destructive influence was that of his older sister Natalia, who introduced him to narcotics at the age of twelve, and who was to die of an overdose.

After the 1917 Revolution he moved to Yalta with his father where he was to experience some of the horrors of the Civil War and where his literary career was to begin. In 1919 they both moved to Constantinople and then on to Paris in 1921. He was soon—possibly having been driven from Paris because of his mother's imminent arrival—to be part of the Russian scene in Berlin from 1922–24, where he studied art. His return to Paris may have been triggered by the revaluation of the mark, which meant the end of the high standard of living enjoyed by expatriate Russians during that brief period. Paris is the city with which he is most readily associated. Here he divided his time between sport, writing, art, philosophy and theology. From this point on, apart from a few half-hearted attempts to earn a living, he adopted the life of an impoverished artist surviving on the minimum. Thus he was to live out ten short years. Gleb Struve made the scathing comment that Poplavsky 'did not know how to work and did not want to work', and though it is certainly true that Poplavsky never held down a paying job for more that a few days at a time, as a writer, considering his short life, he was extremely productive. The Poplavsky of this period was known famously for the dark glasses that he rarely took off and he fits in with the French tradition of the *flâneur*—the writer who ambles along the Parisian streets absorbing sights and sounds of everything around him. However, he was seen by many as a brief flame too rapidly extinguished. During his short life, although he published only one book of poems, *Flags* (1931), he commanded great respect both amongst his peers, and also the older generation. Volumes of his poetry published posthumously were: *Snowy Hour* (1936), *From a Garland of Wax* (1938) and *Airship of an Unknown Direction* (1965). He also completed one novel, *Apollon Bezobrazov*, and started another, *Homeward from Heaven*, as well as writing extensive journals.

Poplavsky was to die under mysterious circumstances—seen in various lights as suicide, poisoning, or an accidental overdose—in October 1935. The descriptions of his tragic end may have been glossed over by those wishing to preserve his memory, but the story goes that he ran into a fellow drug addict intent on suicide, who somehow involved the poet. He died from an overdose of narcotics which may also have had an admixture of some poison. Poplavsky regularly used hard drugs throughout his life, so there was always the risk that he might die in such circumstances. Leonid Livak adds further light on the topic in his discussion of Poplavsky, where he describes his ongoing fascination with death, tracking any available evidence that there is to suggest that Poplavsky may have willingly entered into a suicide pact. Certainly in *Flags* there is a sense that poetically at least he was, like Keats, 'half in love with easeful death'.

Looking at his poetry as a whole, the novel, and at times absurd images which appear in Poplavsky's poetry reflect his affinities with avant-garde movements such as French Surrealism and the Russian

Oberiu. However, it is the poignancy of the poetry that gives it a lasting quality. As his work develops his poetry becomes increasingly personal with Poplavsky a Hamlet-like figure expressing the unbearable pain of living in the world. To reinforce this state of mind he frequently transfers this emotional state onto the natural world itself, 'the life of the woods grow sad on the mountains' and 'where with terrible voices the leaves on the trees / cry out in lament at their terrible destruction'. At the same time it is clear that he is infinitely moved by this natural world, in spite of its bleakness, 'how endlessly touching is the evening'. This ambivalence seems to be part of a search for something transcendent, mixed with fear that perhaps it is a futile hope, expressed either with moving directness, 'Everything now is meaningless and clear / be at peace there is nothing more', or on the edge of despair, 'It's terrible to think how time passes / you can neither think nor live'. One is left feeling, however, not that Poplavsky had a death-wish but more that he was absorbed in a kind of pleasurable melancholy, indeed that such a glorification of melancholy provided him with a purpose. Nikolay Tatishchev, who was instrumental in publishing a great deal of Poplavsky's poetry after his death, tells us: 'Poplavsky loved those overcast Parisian winters and to watch the poor and wealthy and their states of mind.' Many of the poems show Poplavsky as such an outsider, expressing affinities with the various isolated street figures who walk the poems. Poplavsky, both in his poetry and in life, interested himself in a wide range of beliefs. He was however predominantly focused on a traditional Christian God, although his relationship with this God is expressed as a close friendship between two ordinary people: 'I don't believe in God or myself / but I see how fragile we both are' and 'God called to me but I didn't reply, we felt shy and cursed our timidity'.

As far as translation of Poplavsky's poetry is concerned, his wordplay loses much in translation, yet at other times his poems are a gift for the translator: the novel ways in which he personifies nature, the poignant quality of many of his direct statements and the sense of movement in some of his images can all be conveyed into English without great loss. Consider these lines form 'Salome':

> . . . to the song of
> the white acacia, the evening walked away…
> beyond the river and into the clouds.

> ...The restaurant
> orchestra swam over the marsh
> and into the interminable distance.

When we come to look specifically at *Flags* we see many of the above traits but also there is something decidedly unique in this text. There is certainly some indication of a poet at the apprentice stage of his career—occasionally he is a little wordy, and his ideas are sometimes stronger than emotion—but what is infinitely appealing about this first collection is its strangeness: absurd, and sometimes incomprehensible images abound and one has to track the way the poems interact to try to grasp his overall meaning. Fortunately we have the daunting scholarship of Hélène Menegaldo who has committed many years to studying Poplavsky's work, as well as getting as much of his archive into print as possible. Menegaldo offers us the vital key to help us make the journey through the network of symbols in *Flags*:

> A strange fantastic world, full of fairy-tale phantoms, closer to French surrealism than Russian symbolism, a complex work, difficult to understand, however, one where it is possible to trace certain patterns.

From here she provides the reader with an exhaustive examination of Poplavsky' highly individualized symbolic system. Poplavsky's symbolism is attractive because it manages to avoid the rather archaic feel of much Symbolist verse where words become limited to a single hidden meaning which transforms them, in Mandelstam's words, into 'stuffed birds'. What Menegaldo has shown is the way the difficulty inherent in some of the poems in *Flags* is clarified by looking at this system as a whole. She describes how it works by way of a general division between earth, air and water, with the verbs of swimming and flying dominating the poetry:

> In the heavenly heights the poet tries to get in contact with God: in the sea he hopes to return to the source of his existence, but in the earth he is transformed to stone, ice or marble, to dream of other universes.

What is intriguing is not so much these ideas but the endless plasticity with which Poplavsky plays around with them. Menegaldo tracks all the images that associate with the various realms but also shows, interestingly, the way that angels, say, not only inhabit the airy realm but are also like humans and thus they may be trapped on the earth, or lose their powers if they don't get back to the sky before the dawn. Poplavsky does not create a Symbolist sky of otherness, ether and archaic words (a tendency which makes some poetry from the Russian symbolists grate on the modern ear), but one that as readily has cows or packhorses flying there. The air is the place of flight and night dreams, where one can be superior to the sleeping, but it is equally Icarus's dangerous world of chance where there is a risk of falling back into the abyss. Poplavsky's dream world takes him back below the earth where he is forced to encounter gnomes, and sorcerers. His poems are inhabited by various goddesses, each with different traits. Towers, and skyscrapers are important symbols to show the link between earth and sky, and the airship that becomes the title of his final collection is the means whereby one can travel safely to the heights. This symbolic system continues to play a role in his other collections but nowhere is it explored in quite such a surreal way as it is in *Flags*. A likely source for some of the ideas, indeed, may be one of the earliest examples of Surrealist writing, *Maldoror* by Comte de Lautréamont (1846–70; the pseudonym of Isidore Ducasse), outlined here in the blurb for Paul Knight's Penguin translation:

> Maldoror, a master of disguises pursued by the police is the incarnation of evil as he makes his way through the nightmarish realm of angels and gravediggers, hermaphrodites and prostitutes, lunatics and strange children.

Without some of the darker, more sadistic elements of Lautréamont's 'hallucinatory' text, Poplavsky's *Flags* conveys the same sense of whirlwind movement, of flight and swimming through the elements and it is this feel of the reader being carried along on such a journey that is one of the key attractions of *Flags*.

And 'flags' as a symbol is in itself intriguing. This symbol has been attributed to Apollinaire, who had argued that poets should avoid nationalistic flags, and unite under the single flag of art, but, in Poplavsky's case, Menegaldo is once more illuminating. She notes first of all that the ocean has a further significance for him as reminder of his past life, the journey he has already completed and his desire for future travel—thus the boat becomes the means for both physical and spiritual journeys. Menegaldo draws our attention to the flags on the ship in the poem 'Flags' noting how 'the poet can detect the flags' sadness, having dreamed of their former ocean life':

> On a summer day over the white pavement
> Japanese lanterns were hanging.
> The trumpet voice mumbled over the boulevards,
> on big poles the flags were dreaming.
>
> It seemed to them that somewhere the sea was close,
> and along them a wave of heat was running,
> the air slept, not seeing dreams as Lethe.
> Pity of the flags overshadowed us.
>
> The boat's frame appeared to them.
> Black smoke that tenderly flew away,
> and a prayer over the boundless wave
> of the ship's music on Christmas Eve.
>
> The quick flight on the mast in the ocean,
> the noise of salutes, the cry of black sailors,
> and the enormous lowering down over anchors
> in the hour of the fall of the body in mourning clothes.
>
> First the flag glistens over the horizon
> and cheerfully whirls to the flashes of cannons
> and last of all sinks among the debris
> and still with a wing beats about the water.
>
> Like the soul, which leaves the body,
> like my love for You. Answer me!
> How many times did you wish on a summer's day
> to wrap yourself up in a flag and die.

Thus these personified flags have multiple meanings: they are indicators of unknown worlds to which one might travel; symbolic of the lost world of the émigré—both nostalgia for the past and a longing for discovery—and finally even suggestive of the poet's soul.

Poplavsky's later poems become increasingly rich in emotion but this early collection tantalizes in an entirely unique way—Poplavsky's imagination takes us into a variety of other worlds, ranging from the mystical, to the magical, fairy-tale and child-like—a highly original collection.

Belinda Cooke
2009

Eagles

I remember the varnished wings of the carriage,
silence and lies. Fly sunset, fly.
This is how Christopher Columbus hid from the crew
the immensity of the voyage they had made.

The crooked back of the coachman
was encircled with orange glory.
Grey hair curled under the hard hat,
and in the back us, like a two-headed eagle.

I look, my eyes avoiding the sun,
which still manages to dazzle even more:
the powdered implacable beak,
threatens passers-by till they blink and shiver.

You threatened me for eighteen days,
on the nineteenth you softened and faded.
The sunset finally left off playing on the panes:
suddenly it turned noticeably colder.

Autumn smoke rose over the carriage
where our happiness was slow to depart,
but the captain kept from the crew
the immensity of the voyage they had made.

BC/RM

Transformation into Stone

We went out. But the scales inexorably sank.
Such cold scales of twilight,
the snowy hours floated past,
circled on the stones and disappeared.

On the island houses did not move
and cold drifted solemnly over the earthen wall.
It was winter. Doubting Thomas
placed his fingers in its scarlet sunset.

The tracks of heels in the snow
pierced like an umbrella spike, a stiletto.
My purple and steady hand
lay like stone on the bench.

Winter drifted over the city there
where sadly we no longer waited,
just like the sky holds its many towns,
as it spreads itself over the large distance.

BC/RM

'How Cold the Public Waters Are . . .'

'How cold the public waters are,'
You said, and looked below.
The mist flew beyond the stone ledge
where the frozen carts were rumbling along.

Over the roofs three o'clock showed up blue,
we went down to the moraine roadway
and I thought to myself: I shall raise a cry now
like these boat sirens.

But I walked on further and made you laugh,
just like the condemned joke with their executioners:
the tram horse which rushed up, neighing
suddenly became silent and calm behind us.

We parted: well we don't always need to be ashamed
of the closeness that is already long past,
like autumn that's passed along the embankment
never to return on its tracks.

BC/RM

Disgust

The soul was raised in a shelter for the deaf and dumb,
but the defect was cured:
she walks through the wards of the hospital
saying goodbye to everyone she meets.
Having settled in the corner on the tram car
travelling with things to the station
the mother turned her black eyes sternly
on the unfamiliar child.
And since that time how often has she wanted
to become deaf and dumb once more,
when the deathly arrow flew
of words she understood too readily.
Or at least if it were possible to go into service
in that same shelter so that she wouldn't hear
the obscene words of friendship
and the words of love heard so frequently here.

BC/RM

In a Garland of Wax

For Alexander Braslavsky

We cherish our leisure so dear to us
and hide unquestionably from hope,
the bare trees sing in the forest
and the city is like an enormous French horn.

How we love to joke about before the end,
this is something known by the first and last.
For a man disappears more completely then
like an actor with a divine face.

The transparent wind clumsily echoes your words.
And here is the snow. Die away.
Who dares to argue with the inglorious evening,
to warn the silence of the sunset.

October circles, like a whitish hawk—
in the sky we see his grey feathers.
But carved out of alabaster
the sheep-soul sees nothing.

The cold holiday wanes listlessly.
The mist moves on and off the mountain.
I remember, death sang to me in my youth:
do not wait for fate to take you.

BC/RM

Immobility

The day was indifferently windy,
indifferently free of people and airy.
In the mirror I see my wretched jacket
and the bulging vein of my ancestors' forehead.

Diseases of the heart are fatal to me,
I hear my blood surging—death.
But it is as useless to resist it as it is
to block this Thursday crawling in.

The air rocks above me, it flows along
with no definite goal, under the moon
visible in the middle of the day,
merciless boredom in its sights.

And the wind drops down into the fireplace
like a diver into a sunken vessel,
having noticed that one drowned man
is looking recklessly into the empty water.

BC/RM

The Magic Lantern

The evil smoker blows the smoke rings of days,
smoke trails weakly from the ceiling:
perhaps he is some rake or a grave digger
or a soldier from a passing regiment.

Reckless art fascinates my captive mind,
and I then begin to smoke, but suddenly
in the thick air my mind begins to fade,
and only the pipe on the armchair burns.

Tobacco country drifts and drifts
under the sun of the small lampshade.
One moment I am endlessly happy,
the next I am wheezing, I take myself to task.

It is pleasant to build a smoky firmament.
This is an inglorious conquest.
Spring drifts, spring slips into summer,
life moves backwards carelessly to death.

BC/RM

Joint Reign
To Yuri Rogal-Levitsky

The sabre of death whistles in the haze,
it hacks off our heads and souls.
On the mirror's glass the warm steam
carves our past and our future.

And the sparrows of mischievous dreams
ride the teeming mind.
And from the sun-filled apparition
the brain flows onto the earth like wax.

The damaged vessel bleeds
with both black and white blood.
The unequal halves of the body
on two catafalques.

And I am buried in two cemeteries,
departing beneath the earth and into heaven,
and two goddesses with whom I am in love
perform two different rites.

BC/RM

An Attempt with Inadequate Means
To Ilya Zdanevich

A garland of sonnets will help me to live,
I write straightaway, but find no genuine help,
how quickly the edge of the ravine creeps around.
A twitching at the elbow runs onto the writing paper.

The bear's den of the soul is empty,
there is a bottle and a newspaper lying there.
In the city zoo, like the eternal Jew
the owner walks over the twigs of the jail.

Our life is amusement for the ages,
with power beyond man
submerged in the prison of fate.

Only five steps remain for the race,
five iambs, the tormenting bliss of words
so the wild beast should not forget freedom.

BC/RM

In a Struggle with the Snow

The white snow is only just above the white house,
it barely sounds or appears to be white.
I arrived at two, I really did . . . but found nothing,
just got stiff with cold. Nothing to be done.

This game of words could break a donkey,
but I am an iron donkey made of jelly.
I always felt pity yet I've turned to jelly,
I've become so weak—please have pity on me.

I don't remember, but I really must try. No I shall die.
The snow will melt. The house will sink to no purpose
as the familiar car crashes in the abyss and night speeds
towards morning—to destruction in the morning.

But once more I ring at the main entrance.
They meet me. Vera, I still have hope
that my icy campaign will end, but You are dead.
You have been dead for a long time . . . I miss you.

BC/RM

Army Stanzas

To Alexander Ginger

Just like the off duty soldier looks at himself
in the mirror, at the barrack gates
we saw our regal attire reflected in God
and slowly turned back.

Sacred Church Scripts—we know army regulations.
But we stood on guard duty, but then
lay down tired. The madness
of friendship gave us up to the enemy.

We pass. The parade of prisoners passes,
the soles of their feet beating on the firm snow.
We march the width and length and breadth
of the universe; but perhaps we do it in a dream.

But now the guns pound in the distance,
the ambulances are jostled about.
And on the road, as on soft wax,
the mysterious ruts are visible.

The rain breathes like a carthorse.
In the heavens its sides are glittering.
Whose are these tears? We walk in our rubber boots.
Say goodbye to the base, we are going. See you later.

Clouds track us, march out of step.
It is so fine. Things will no longer get worse.

BC/RM

Rain

To Vladimir Sveshnikov

The tent swelled, like a striped sail.
The sleepy people came out of the church,
inexplicably the wind suddenly went into a rage
then calmed down. It is a swindler and a cheat.

Around us, as in a heavenly garden,
the laurels rocked in round tubs,
and loudly, but inexpressibly sweetly
the gramophone sounded, like Orpheus in hell.

'My poor friend, live for a quarter of your life.
A quarter of hope is enough,
a quarter of reprisal for the crime
and a quarter of fear before one's eyes close.

I do want this. I am happy when I choose.
I am free to be a black light in the darkness,
I refuse to take from anything,
I refuse to live on that earth'.

It was already evening in the depths of the tavern
where we withered like flowers.
The rays climbed to the pinnacle of the world
and smiling they died there.

At times, it seemed the rain would stop.
I don't recall which of us quietly got up
and listened for a long time as the bell
at the cinema entrance rang for the first sitting.

BC/RM

Sentimental Demonology
To Mikhail Larionov

Day descended, in extreme decline,
and the finger of rain turned the transparent globe around.
God called me but I didn't reply.
We felt shy and cursed our timidity.

We exchanged greetings. We parted. This said
I walk into the club: I look for the devil there where the cards are.
Ah here he is. I introduce myself haughtily. I'm such a fool.
And the devil replies I know you from school.

You remember, when on a cold day
you were skiing out of town,
I am the curly-headed governor from Paris
who told some crude story.

When you were sitting in the tram, in a dream,
an exercise book hugged to your chest without a blotter,
I being the conductor didn't ask for a ticket,
gloating under my official blue cap.

When you were in the park alone with a young girl
silent and turning red from shyness,
a puny gentleman sat next to you
in his buttoned up official's overcoat.

Or in the dead hour, when the night owl travels
through the cold of morning, neither drunk nor sober,
the cabman with his unperturbed passenger
flew right into you with a terrible crashing.

Or in the endless street, where the tap
of feet floundered on the moon's fork,
I approached you softly, as in a forest,
walking next to you noiselessly in a circle.

And at that moment when the wagon rolling along
suddenly speeded up
the face beside your loved one
glanced without expression.

Face to face and then face to face again,
up to the very death and to death itself,
everywhere scoundrel meets scoundrel
dressed in a dressing gown or even dressed as a lady.

Until, coldly, chokingly, death decides to lies down
on the chest, like a lady in a coat,
and indifferently the chauffeur-archangel
crushes the reptile with his pink car.

BC/RM

The Angels of Hell
To Aleksey Arapov

I tell you, it is all the same to me: I am happy.
The wind breathes above me, the scoundrel.
And the sun shows little interest
as it floods the forest abundantly with light.

Whales play hide and seek with the boats.
And in the depths a sea serpent hides.
Trams soar up to the mountain
and the door clatters, like corpses on coffins.

And the days pass like prisoners' tambourines,
there where the cemetery of Clubs lies.
Tsars sit like fat pedants
while valets hold sticks and knives.

And the ladies—how beautiful these ladies are,
one with a kerchief, another with a flower,
a third with an apple offering it to Adam
stuck in the throat like our Adam's apple.

Rustling, they enter the house of cards,
they nod with fans in their hands.
They bring their destructive fashion with them:
deception and poison in an orange stocking.

The silk skirts of the tickets rustle
gold rings like a kiss. Cigars, eyes and pipes
are burning in the darkness—suddenly there is a shot!
It's like the dance-master at the ball.

The stool is tipped over. Worms creep out,
while the cheat is caught with a fistful of spades,
and under the lamp the banker continues
to deal for peace, green light and dust.

BC

A Struggle with Sleep

While a cow is flying in the sky
little dogs are on light wings.
We turned up at half past one
and we let out a deep breath.

Oh the days pass by so quickly under the window,
just like cyclists—You and I alone
like a musical sign, keep a close eye
on the happenings outside.

The to and fro of the fingers of notes
strive to touch us: such hooks!
You violin up there, are the curved horned one,
while I below am the round bass key.

The various notes are like the notes of governments,
but fate got tired of sitting at the piano.
The exercise book slammed shut: bang! No harm done.
We fell asleep in the dark in the tormented nights.

Midnight electric light sun crawls along the page,
dirty white like snow. I have a dream:
we abandoned the music-stand, a dream!
Dressing like people, we went out. We are no more.

There is only a pair of steps between the violin and bass,
But the stave runs through the restaurant. Or rather the wall.
We chat through the fence just like at our neighbours' dachas,
but both inaccessible and within reach like truth.

BC

An Imitation of Zhukovsky

The naked maiden arrives and drowns,
the impossible tree is sighing in a tunic.

The fire-spitting train descended into the blue valley
of the glass, it sank underneath the glacier.

The blue, watery world crawls along safely,
the bit does not chafe the silent, freezing ox.

A most dangerous dream is flying free of charge.
Enraptured, it is violet and sweet.

Approach, come, unnatural enemy
irretrievable and drowsy, my comrade cancer.

Send out a distant but distinct sound,
under which I, a most tender bear am dancing.

The big wall recoils a little
and like a snake is creeping.

But all the same that world is like a finger in an enormous ring
or like a round hat on a villain.

Or like the maiden who slowly enters and drowns,
there where the tree breathes bitterly in a tunic.

BC

Spring in Hell
To George von Guk

It was on that evening, on that evening.
The houses began to boil like teakettles.
Through the windows burst the bubbling of love.
And 'love is not a potato'
and 'your bare shoulders'
spun round in the terrifying waltz,
they flew and sang like lions.
There was a sudden crash by the porch and the bell began to bark.
Spring went silently up the stairs.
And everyone suddenly remembered they were lonely.
Each shouted I am alone—suffocating from low spirits.
And in the singing of the night and the roar of the morning,
in the toneless bubbling of the evening in the park,
the dead years got up out of their death bed
and carried the bed like postage stamps.
The river was rocking like a sea of asphalt.
The motorboats rose and fell,
the sharks of trams having caught sight of the enemy
released fountains into the nostril of the corridors.
And it wasn't terrible to rise up onto the crest
to rush without looking back on the waves of the crowd
and to sense destruction in the raspberry sky
and sweet weakness and the passion of weakness.
On that evening, on that evening described in books,
it wasn't terrible for us to make a din in the wind.
The buildings were aslant and full of cracks.
They fell, like a freshly struck-down corpse
and were full of happiness, although they lacked knowledge.
The air beat with wings in the milky window
there, where stretching out immortal hands
spring circled like a dancer on fire.

BC

Don Quixote
To Sergei Sharshun

We need to dream. We need to feel delight.
We need to give in. We do not need to live.
Because the row of columns shines beneath the moon,
Africans are singing and the propeller drones.

Don Quixote's horse flies up onto the porch
along with scented Sancho on a red donkey.
And suddenly they appear in the night, like poetry or a hiccup:
the parade, the ballet and the pointless races.

The hands of the ragged windmills applaud
and merchants shout with Madonnas' voices,
some loser leaps over the roofs of the banks,
while courteous Faust and sacred Cupid are dancing.

Once again on the round-shouldered horse hump
in the moonlit evening opera he weeps, he sleeps,
the water nymph's hands stretch out to the sleeping one,
the lilac-blue shafts of her fingers are streaming.

On the airy swings, in yards, in threads
a rider, a fat man, and a mule rise,
and shameless postcards pour from the sky
(and starving poets make wry faces in their sleep).

But with an ink knife, with a lilac chopper,
the sharp cloud chops off the fingers to the moon
and broken away, like rags of poisonous wadding
holy fools are floundering, through a false wilderness.

And hooves strike with all their might on the ice.
Shivering, the worn out nags come to a halt.
The honest magician, the lilac pole is sleeping,
immortal ice is shining like a white coat.

In detestable bliss the transparent rocks
turn violet as they melt beneath the false ray of light,

and in the ice the frozen shark-girls are sleeping
shining like silk with their sloping shoulders.

And our traveller wit stands in an awkward pose,
a motionless sextant in his blue hand.
Narrowing his lifeless eyes, he smiles into the sky,
like seeing the Northern Cross for the first time.

And on the white snow, as on a soft bed,
the hero of adventure lay, this batman was sprawled,
and it seemed to him that he was in a marble bath,
and all around were orchids and African style.

And all the sky buzzed and howled over the sleeping,
street lamps were burning, the shaft of the searchlight crawled.
There the airship flew, the cleanly shaven snob
indifferently spun its glittering snout.

And fine ladies were looking through the windows
as the oval shadow was flying along the plain.
Motors burst out laughing, monocles tumbled
and the industrial day rose over the wilderness.

BC

The negative pole is silent and shines . . .
To Grigori Reshotkin

The negative pole is silent and shines.
It competes with no-one. It is the ocean.
The dead man sleeps in delightful blue peace,
returned by fate in the absolute night.

With a head toppled over to the black sky,
with the motionless grin of teeth worn away,
he no longer dreams of countries he hasn't been to,
soaring absolutely in the motionless glass.

At such a depth the current dies down
and words start to become indistinct in the distance.
At such a depth our studies come to an end,
as do military service and the sailor's life.

The machine leads the singing in the electric tower
and the light gives out an enormous beam
and the deafened people with enormous lips
lean towards happiness along with the vessel.

And the searchlight lies on the smooth water
and for half a minute burns under the water.
The metal house, as though it was the bell of spirits
sinks silently ringing in the blueness.

And the iceberg floats by over the place of the wreck
like Venus de Milo in white tights.

BC

Astral World
To Olga Kogan

Happiness clears itself of any hope,
our house flaps its tiled wings,
and walks like a bird. Be amazed you fools:
come and visit us when we go out.

On the tall balcony, over past and future,
we sit without waistcoats and chew silently.
A passenger monster rises between the stars,
rushes up and we fly away together.

The air gives a whistle. The airless stairwell is silent.
Here the earth drops in the inky pocket.
Button up your light shirt mechanic.
Here is Venus, and we abandon the carriage.

The world is muddle-headed and divides into four.
We walk, we crawl, take wing and doze;
we meet bored ladies and gentlemen,
we live and want to return to earth.

But the mysterious world is like water from a tap
that pushes us, but then disappears through our fingers.
I fling myself towards You, but the stylish hall
lights up, and I am before the white screen,

before the blue water, where there is a round fish,
before the air: the air revolves, like a ball.
And over us spirits walk like black icebergs.
And there Your soul shall be.

Big forests sink from the sky.
And with a whistle gigantic grasses grow.
Dew flows as a terrible waterfall.
And the grasshopper rattles like a train. You are right.

It's time for us. We breathe, are startled and flap our wings.
We circle like the hand of a clock, like a squirrel on a clock.

We walk into the restaurant where the evil lackey,
on guard, is surly as he takes our coats.

And like a fine bright rose
we light up a cigarette.

BC

Paysage d'enfer
To George Storm

The water curled and sighed dully,
the water flew over me in the haze,
the soul was silent on the border of sound,
just like the snow will fall decidedly to earth.

But in the blue sea, where birds are diving
while I the drowned man float prepared,
the red-faced evening bathes for a long time
among the water plants of the town gardens.

The shell roofs were glittering,
the train sagged, like a sea-serpent,
and higher up, that is to say further, closer, lower,
the eccentric airship roamed like a fish.

The jellyfish clouds barely shone,
in dispute with untimely death
and I walked importantly with a sailor's walk
over solid ground to the far side of the boat.

And everything was in the shallows,
where bright light still reaches.
Here we sink, here we stand on the bottom.
And a copper gramophone sings greetings to us.

In the depths of the speeding sea
drowned friends met each other.
and slowly we notice on the plateau
the dawn is already bearing new corpses.

The water breathes and circles softly
like life, that is the gentle dream of God
and the ball of wind speeds across the field,
to drop into a billiard pocket, like a letter at the post office.

BC

A Starlit Hell

Listen. The mad star sings over the drowsy garden
imitating the nightingale.
Angels are silent descending from the airship,
they come onto the ice with a favourable smile.

In the tropical night, over the ship,
the star burned with a green flame.
The one standing at the helm turned pale,
a female passenger became lost in concentration of the sky.

Wandering in the sounds over the mountain she flamed up,
where the glass boy slept in a snowy dress,
he started to cry but did not open his eyes,
and melted at dawn in tender smoke.

It seemed to her that she was flowering in hell.
She circles at the nighttime ball.
She lies among defeated souls
like a paper star on the floor.

And suddenly she woke; cold floated in the bushes,
she was shining, on the hand of Christ.

BC

To Arthur Rimbaud

No one knows
what time it is
and they don't want
to be silent in a dream.

The carriage shifts to the left
The whistle sings.
And the empty east
turns red.

Oh, Oh Virgin Mary
forgive me
I met Eve
in a foreign country.

The green gaslight
dazzled the passers-by.
She was
like You.

The café-chantant
made some meaningless noise
and the fountain spluttered
unceasingly.

London was full
of a crowd of fools
and Rimbaud is ready
to go to the Congo.

Among greasy dress-coats
and commotions
we were sitting
at a dish of lobster.

The knee of his trousers
was glittering
and Verlaine
had a red nose.

And suddenly along the stage
along the heads
having lifted her knees
Goddess Anna

comes strutting,
goodness in evil
desired of souls
God on a donkey.

Oh forgotten day . . .

Smashing people
As though they were dishes,
the donkey kicked me
with his hooves.

But I was unable to wipe clean
the mark of the blow
and could not fly away
from the boa-constrictor.

Oh maiden, your young
face has died.
Your full moon double
has risen.

Were you real
Goddess of the heavens?
I have even forgotten
your name.

I walk alongside a horse
in the whitish night
with the smile of a corpse
and a cigarette.

BC

The Black Madonna
To Vadim Andreyev

The days turned blue, turned lilac,
dark, fine, empty.
On the trams the people became drowsy,
their sacred heads were bowed,

their heads rocked happily.
The asphalt was sleeping, where mid-day was spying,
and it seemed, in the air, in the sadness,
every moment that the train was moving away.

There was a string of cheap lights,
and the cheerful bustle of people,
and in the poor, deserted, clearing
the clarinet and violin started to die out.

And once again, before that very grave,
they utter and give birth to that magic sound.
And both musicians will be paid
with black beer from sweaty hands.

Then the cavalry will pass through indifferently,
dressed in their red uniforms,
exhausted, not enjoying the holiday,
the artillery well back from the parade.

And to the dust, to eau de cologne, to sweat,
to the noise of the vaulted arch overhead,
the gunpowder smoke of fireworks,
will merge with the smell of vomit.

And the arrogant youth in those immense
bell-bottom trousers, suddenly hears
the brief shot of happiness, instantaneous flight,
the red moon of summer on the waves.

Suddenly from the lips of the trombone
the screech of balls is circling in the haze.

The black Madonna screams wildly
her hands stretched out in a deathly sleep.

And through the nighttime, sacred, hellish heat,
through the lilac smoke, where the clarinet was singing,
the snow, white and merciless, starts to whirl about
going on for millions of years.

BC

Diabolique
To Victor Mamchenko

The people by the columns burst out laughing,
where the moon stood in a strange pose.
The evening had a sharp smell of eau de cologne,
from dancers and the restaurant.

Autumn crept into the middle of summer.
Over the bridges leaves were turning orange.
They carried skeletons on carriages,
orangeries and conservatories.

And in a fine descending scale
the heat was snoring on its belly on the roadway,
it looked at ladies' legs,
covered smart trousers with dust.

People became irritated and without getting tanned
they slowly gave themselves up to the stifling heat.
Towards evening a second heat arrived,
the souls expected a third at night.

But the long-wished lilac darkness
unlocked minds and, parted lips.
The dandyish youth without horns or a tail
started to whistle to the maid.

And in the lilac aura, aura,
eternally fine and wretched
into the sky appeared Laura Laura
and a singer behind her in red tights.

The black kettledrums beat a hollow sound,
the choir of Erina answered in the abyss,
and July like Faust on a centaur,
dissipated dead heat in the darkness.

But confusion of spirits is sudden,
the wind reduces the garden to its knees,

our ears catch the sound of soft laughter,
its hollow sound rises above the train station:

Helen Queen of horrors.

And behind her Apollos of Troy,
with golden birds in their hands,
rose in a scarlet halo
the dark tracks of blood in the clouds.

And the moon sings of a snow-filled paradise
and the billow of inky black clouds was swaying
and playing with the next phrase,
thunder fell on the black arsenal.

And in the sudden flying flame
as on a pink shell, she
seemed to us peacefully sleeping
with the foam on golden waves.

BC

The Last Parade
To Lydia Kharlampiyevne Pumpianskaya

The summer day was full of the noise of happiness,
the lightning glittered like a blue bird.
Fantastic chariots
came out from the fire station.

And through the town under children's escort,
under the bravura roar of flabby trumpets
the best of the music hall troupes
passed by in youthful pose.

On the wide backs of skewbald horses
white ballerinas were dozing,
and with a smile athletes
lifted empty weights on a carriage.

The sun warmed the dried plush,
and ugly, drunken faces were watching out of shadowy inns,
their great pink souls
smiled at the passing music.

There was in the crowd the pretty bright rustle,
the glimmer of spring holiday costumes,
drunks shouted from the white arch.
The garden smiled, having decided at last to flower.

The night approached and clowns appeared.
The company burst out laughing at the happiness of life.
Musician horses circled
with golden dragonflies on their rumps.

But then the light flashed in the passage,
lions gave a roar rising up on to their hind legs.
As on an ocean-going steamer
people fight in an ocean of smoke.

And from all sides embraced with the flame
the young tender American

for free, on a curved horn, played
a peaceful funeral waltz.

And then fell and suffocated.
And the great fire is spreading.
It touched the clouds with its stamens
and then in the dawn haze melted.

And in the morning in the halo's intense heat
over the theatre that had walked off into eternity,
the garden opened up in a pink wall
in the empty irreproachable heavens.

BC

At Dawn

To Valerian Driakhlov

The pinkish ghost of dawn
appeared over the tall edifice.
The streetlamps went out in the damp garden,
I prayed to love . . . Light up,
with your serene illumination.

Along the humpbacked bridge in the darkness
the tall people passed by.
And in pursuit of departing spring,
the harsh whistle of nightingale preludes
flew on the horse free of charge.

And in the forest on the untrampled grass,
spring was dying in the darkness.
It smelt of damp, moss and mint.
And the hermit in a shabby fur coat
washed himself in cold water.

BC

Mercy

Sun-filled light, I touched you, but you did not notice,
you did not wake, but simply smiled in your sleep.
Strangely the final dreams were silent at dawn
clandestine, pink snow soared in the air.

Angels flew away from the bosom of the earth
wearied in a night it was time to sleep.
The whole night they were singing in a different world,
but sleeping people did not hurry but moved backwards.

In early morning the coolness is shining
sleeping faces are stained with high colour.
They wash and clean the threshold of hell
and the gates of paradise are closing.

The youth is cherished by his tender wife,
stroked with a transparent maiden's hand.
My friend, are You faithful to a cruel one? I am indeed!
Faith in her will provide You with peace.

The pink wind of the delayed sunset
tenderly strokes me by the hand.
My final peace, my scarlet evening
I feel your kiss on the cheek.

Silently I go dressed in flowers,
ever since childhood I have been ready to die.
Don't study my tracks
I will charge the wind to remove them.

BC

The rose-coloured hour floated over the dawning world . . .

The rose-coloured hour floated over the dawning world.
The souls returned from paradise to their bodies.
You walked away in your supernatural world.
The sun rose, and the candle on the table went out.

The rose-coloured snow subsided in the peaceful height.
Suddenly You woke again; but You didn't recognise anyone,
Your strange glance stole in astonished and tender
and wallowed in the half darkness of the high hall.

And beyond the window, never to be forgotten glistening with dew,
summer blossomed and the gardens sank into the river.
And along the road, his scythe glistening in the sun
death walked away and the devil ran away travelling light.

The never to be forgotten world was shining taken in by summer.
Steam rose into the sky with white clouds,
and athletes raising their ancient hands
broke stones and slept in the heat's embrace.

The sun was shining in immortal fascination.
The flags were rising, the crowd started to shout.
Something terrible hid itself in this radiance.
It wanted to throw itself to the ground, to forget, to fall silent.

BC

Dolorosa

On the balcony sunset was weeping
in a bright red fancy dress gown.
And the elegant evening in uniformed frock-coat
bent over it to no purpose.

And then over the lace lattices
it rose to him, and suddenly,
he gave out a short groan like a tram
and he threw down the sickly looking corpse.

And then on the street, in the square,
under the transparent battle of hours, around the corner,
a light blue horse ran out,
a blue carriage of glass.

Loudly slamming the musical carriage door,
autumn sprang down in motion,
and having pressed its hand to its sick heart
raised a cry like they shout in hell.

And in reply from the air from the darkness
swarms of white roses flew,
and winter, under the strange sign of Cancer,
departed into the sky to dissipate the frost.

And dancing under the ball of the streetlamp
subsiding in the bottomless silence,
death began to sing totally for free
over the Madonna lying on the earth.

BC

The Rose of Death
To George Ivanov

In the black park we met the spring,
a cheap violin softly played out of tune.
Death came down on a hot-air balloon
touched those in love on the shoulder.

Evening is pink, the wind carries roses.
On the fields the poet draws a picture.
Evening is pink, the roses smell of death
and the green snow falls onto the branches.

The dark air showers stars,
nightingales sing, echoing motors,
and the tubercular gaslight blazes
in the kiosk over the green sea.

Boats depart in the starry sky,
spirits wave with kerchiefs on the bridge,
and glittering through the dark air
the steamer sings on the viaduct.

The obscure town runs away into the mountains.
Night makes a noise in the ballroom
and soldiers leaving the town
drink thick beer at the station.

Low, low, brushing against souls,
the moon's ball floats over the booth,
and from the boulevard over the frail organ
the carousel waves to the ladies.

And spring endlessly rose-coloured
smiling, receding into the firmament,
unfolds the dark-blue fan
with the distinct inscription: death.

BC

The delightful evening was full of smiles and sounds . . .

The delightful evening was full of smiles and sounds,
the light blue moon floated by high-sounding,
in the half darkness you stretched your immortal hand towards me,
that unforgettable hand that drowsily fell from a shoulder.

This evening was strangely heavy and secretly oppressive,
recoiling the sunset left the lights in the heights,
and large flowers decomposing in beds like souls
shone dying and heavily breathed in sleep.

You encircle me delightfully with a slow glance,
and settling back fell asleep, went back to sleep.
I saw how the angel traveller in a crumpled spring dress,
in a mysterious pose admired hell.

And spring died and the moon returned to the sun.
The sun rose and a dark blush appeared.
Over the polluted park the sacred vision was missing.
The world rose again and started to cry and shed its blossom with rose-
      coloured snow.

BC

The Moonlit Airship

I want to destroy you,
I want to be destroyed,
about the fine death of souls
I will tell you in hell.

The angel builds a palace on the moon,
the airship departs in sleep.
The crosses of the propellers break into song,
the leaves of flowers drop off.

The blue sound cuts the ether,
the dead world is approaching.
The moonlit port comes to light,
the young devil is smiling.

And immense in the darkness
the row of columns descends into the water
in the bluest of blue rays of the moon
the row of colonnades resounds in the darkness.

In the emerald nighttime water
the fine faces of young girls are sleeping,
and in the shadows of light blue columns
the stone Apollo dozes.

Gardens break into blossom in the fire.
White castles ascend like smoke,
and darkly through the small blue wood,
the dark sand burns brightly.

Flowers are singing in the garden.
The statues of souls come to life.
And like butterflies from the flame
words reach me.

Believe me, angel, the moon is high,
musical clouds

surround her, lights
there resound and days shine.

The blue angel fell in love with the spring.
Black light go away and sleep.
Come to love this wretched life.
Take a sip of destruction.

Quietly the skull looks through the window.
In this room it is completely dark,
only silent at the very bottom
a curved shadow sleeps on the wall.

BC

Manuscript Found in a Bottle

We escaped from the Cape of Good Hope, with much hope,
but the sea turned black, and the red sunset of coldnesses
stood over the stern, where the passengers were weeping,
and the ghost of the Titanic accompanied us among blocks of ice.

The drawn out dinner-time gong banged out in the twilight.
In the hall the orchestra started to sing about irretrievable love.
Wandering St Elmo's Fire blazed up on the mast.
The sailors crossed themselves three times in the hold.

We were perishing in mysterious southern seas,
the waves lashed washing away chaise-longues and lifeboats.
We kissed, the boat was sinking in the darkness.
The prisoner shouted in the hold, rattling his stocks.

The helmsman disappeared overboard in a lifeboat,
shots rang out, squeals burst out when struck.
We kissed and over Your head
rockets went out, soaring finely for free.

We two remained on the empty boat,
we became absorbed, but absorbed in happiness.
In the pink dawn a boundless reservoir flamed.
With tears we greeted our new home.

The sun rose over your curly head,
you woke and your hand stirred a little.
In the hold, diving I encountered a dead limb.
Dear corpse, you fed us for a week.

Dear one, we are dying, nestle up to me.
The sky oppresses us, the blue firmness smothers us.
Dear one, we are waking it is a dream
Dear one it isn't true. Dear one, it is death.

The last blush gently rises on Your cheeks.
The inexpressibly happy souls will return to sleep.

Foreigner read the manuscript in the bottle,
and envy us who are with the gods and the stars.

BC/RM

Hamlet

'Hamlet, you are going, stay with me,
we are touching earth, weeping, we shall fall asleep from sadness.
We take pleasure at tears in the humiliation of earth's sadness
we shall cry for sadness, such as we have never before.

Hamlet, you know love warms the snow,
you will touch earth and will whisper: "Forget about everything!"
The moon will stick out its golden horns,
dawn will show pink over the house, where we'll sleep.'

Hamlet replies to her: Forget about me,
for there enormous birds float over me,
softly enormous flowers are blossoming in the flame,
unforgettable faces smile at them.

Blue souls are revolving in pale blue dreams,
the rose-coloured bridge floats over the lilac sea.
Softly from there angels call to the living
to life, fine, inexplicable and new.

There on the great height the frost is blooming,
the young man is sleeping on the height of the pinkish mountain
the garden floats in a crimson flow of roses,
air is dawning, and the pole glitters bluish.

Silently a snowflake falls like a scarlet butterfly,
little jets of flame are quietly flowing on the buildings
but dissolving in the cold sky of Valhalla,
Hamlet disappears before approach of day.

'Hamlet, you are leaving, stay with me!'
the mad girl sang beneath the moon.

BC/RM

Flags

On a summer day over the white pavement
Japanese lanterns were hanging.
The trumpet voice mumbled over the boulevards,
on big poles the flags were dreaming.

It seemed to them that somewhere the sea was close,
and along them a wave of heat was running,
the air slept, not seeing dreams as Lethe
pity of the flags overshadowed us.

The boat's frame appeared to them.
Black smoke that tenderly flew away,
and prayer over the boundless wave
of the ship's music on Christmas Eve.

The quick flight on the mast in the ocean,
the noise of salutes, the cry of black sailors,
and the enormous lowering down over anchors
in the hour the body falls in mourning clothes.

First the flag glistens over the horizon
and to cheerfully whirls to the flashes of cannons
and last sinks among the debris
and still with a wing beats about the water.

Like the soul, which leaves the body,
like my love for You. Speak to me!
How many times did you wish on a summer's day
to wrap yourself up in a flag and die.

BC/RM

Mystic Rondo 1
Tatiana Shapiro

White cottage, I saw you
from the window.
Perhaps Ovid lives in you
and the spring.
At mid-day softly from the white tower
comes a human dream.
The dandy passes in a pink shirt
of the town.
The silk of the sand whistles and becomes quiet.
Resins are breathing.
The distant shot reaches us
like a pigeon.
Hands are sleeping, scarcely touching me.
The sleepy voice
reaches us from the tower
praises the sun.
'Golden souls are sleeping in the sun
of those who believe.
They whisper softly to the heart about the future
from behind the door.
Oh Tristan come past the centuries
and heed
I love you inexplicably
beyond the earth.
You speak to me of happiness from the moon,
happiness—death.
I shall wait for you in the sun
Be firm.'
Resins breathe hotly. Everything passes.
The hand sleeps. On the tower the angel sleeps.
The little white paddle steamer between the trees,
makes a noise with its painted wheel.

BC/RM

Roman Morning

Spring is singing, the blue tit flies to the mountains.
Horses are running in the hippodrome.
The legionnaire is sad at the entrance in the town.
The slave Epictetus is silent in his corner.

Under the green dwarfish acacias
water is rushing into the apertures of cracks,
and glancing into the blueness, where stars are glimmering
spirits are chattering about their business.

Along the pale century old grey road
the car of the senator glides past.
The lilac is glittering. A sailor shouts from the galley
Christ flies into the distance in an aeroplane.

The goddess enters in the twilight into the tower.
From the enormous tower softly the flag twirls about.
Christ having spread out a page of yesterday's paper
sleeps in the air with a star in his hair.

And in the marble cathedral dogs are barking
and statues play on the piano,
ages do not wish to come out of the bath house,
the hand of the moon glistens on the blanket.

And Epictetus sings. My fate
will efface Rome, like clouds the morning.

BC/RM

Mystic Rondo II

It was hot. The flags silently were flapping.
Trumpets were blaring.
Hecuba's watch
had stopped.

Night dropped from the tower
to us on the yard.
In the terrible distance
conversation was audible.

On the granite viaduct
spirits spoke,
that below in hell bodies are in bad spirit,
losing their memories.

On the tall bright red tower
the angel sang,
and in the green sky, terrifying to children
the black airship flew.

Softly the sun travelled along the rails
that became hot.
From the tower the angel sang of dead Elsa
with a distant voice . . .

Of the fine death in the hour of victory,
in the hour of crowning,
of crowning with the sun of dead Ada
of the silence

And the snowy castle could be seen though
in the heart of summer
and the enormous beach on the shores
of Lethe . . .

BC/RM

The Goddess of Life

The moon's ball flew over the fortified roofs,
the unearthly square slept in the sun,
flowers were shining in front of the black recesses.
In the shadows the golden horse was dreaming.

And far below descended with an air of importance
the blue slabs of some sort of stairs.
The goddess of life on the top of the tower
looked in the distance with the smile of Heraclitus.

And there the lilac was flowing, bent over the marble,
and it was stormy in the spring blueness.
The days loitered, like a gypsy camp,
there was dawn, and the park and Sunday.

Where boats sank in the snowy smoke
on the deck trumpets played in a chorus,
through a dream of leaves the dancers passed.
Night finished and the mountains turned blue.

Over the stop the cloud turned scarlet,
the car glided past, hooting wearily, the trumpet dreamed.
The pink-cheeked angel tried to dance clumsily
as the ball drew to a close.

When it burned, smoking, the paper lantern
and the nightingale in the next park sighed.
and in the roses floated the damp dawn cold.
the orchestra faded out, returning to God, blowing the alarm.

Already a new day was beginning beyond the power
of the nighttime spring, unearthly storm.
It was a summer holiday full of the noise of happiness.
and in the lilac sky airships were singing.

Cannons fired into a sea of white smoke.
In the rustling of tennis courts girls are sweating

and in the booths children drank beer
and wanted to wave with a small hand.

And in the distance where there is a castle of red slabs
death dreamed, a curly-haired Heraclitus.

BC/RM

The Death of the Children
To Monsieur Bloom

The sunset turns pink over the snowbound world.
The lilac voice of the moon is rising.
Over the trams, in the horns of the electric lyre
a spark jumps in the dark air of winter.

High over the houses, over the towers of windows,
the greyish snow flies by in sleep
a lilac curl spilled into the side street,
winter is sleeping and in sleep makes way for spring.

The leaden rose of silence is blooming—
the dream of children and the senseless whisper of the gods,
but over the stone vault of the night frost
the whisper of the girl's lightest steps is audible.

Along the heavenly vault on pink heels
efficient angels are walking in silence,
children play hide and seek with them at midnight,
they hang stars on the Christmas tree of the soul.

On the bear's tail a small star rolls down.
Children sat on hares, rushed after it,
and having woken the next day are crying without restraint,
they don't wish to look at earthly toys.

Christmas is blossoming over the bosom of sadness.
Holiday, holiday what are you? I am an alien, I am above the stars.
A chorus of candles in the dining room began to sound in reply,
the astonished little girl grew up.

And when over the window, over the extinguished Christmas tree,
the violet voice of the moon started to sound
the children opened the window of the attic
and slowly threw themselves from the windowsill to sleep.

BC/RM

Hamlet's Childhood

Many children gathered this night on the bridge.
The blue stars put on lemon yellow hats.
The she bear hid her claws in her soft paw,
the boy put on his new sailor's costume.

This bridge softly rocked between life and death,
and there on one side, was the cold dawn.
The black lamplighter carried the head of night on a pole,
reluctantly the gaslight caught fire under the roofs.

The winter morning scratched itself under the snowy feather bed.
and on the other side was sheer lilac forest.
Above called the invisible brilliance of the nightingale.
Bright boats dropped through the leaves from the heavens.

In the air of the town the yellow roofs were burning.
a strange blue sky turned dark in the distance.
People on all floors smiled, glittered.
Only below the earth could not be seen.

A train of pretty wagons rose through a dream,
strange people from the windows waved handkerchiefs.
In the blue glacier an orchestra played waltzes.
Someone talked with the clouds from the balloons.

Each was silent and beautiful and infinitely clever.
The bright dragon taught them about God on the Mount.
In the town Monday was snowy and sleepy,
it was necessary to go to the school at dawn.

Someone was whispering to the children above the bridges.
The children were silent; they turned back from the lights.
The strange conductor gave each of them tickets with crosses,
the alarm clock happily barked at those who returned.

BC/RM

The little girl returned, the angel began to sing ...
To Mikhail Osipovich Tsvetlin

The little girl returned, the angel began to sing at random.
The rain began to drum on wooden instruments.
The little girl returned into hell which was blossoming once more.
Roses smiled at her with their pink lips.

Daddy, see there is a little cat, a dear little cat.
No, darling, it is the sphinx fallen asleep in the meadow.
Daddy, do you see the white chimney sweep?
Little girl I cannot see, little girl I cannot.

Softly the blue stars pass over the town,
their yellow smoke brothers below—the streetlamps.
The stars call them into the sky; there are games and rest,
only they do not wish to go away before dawn.

Gently in the forest white hares are sleeping under roots,
the fir tree rings in the silence with golden rays.
Sleepily in the distance edelweiss friends reply,
softly they wave with their paws at the glaciers.

Night sails and the mountains turn slightly pink.
Angels silently stand on the dawn snow.
Angel save her! The fir tree—I cannot,
let it burn low, I can help it perish.

The white sky blossomed out in the snow, as time,
the ashy day, replaced the pale scarlet daybreak.
The dead fir tree fell on its knees in the snow,
the young woodcutter felled the snow soul.

The dead fir tree went away. Sledges scrape
ironing the road with the green manes of hands,
in the sky was the holiday, there the bright tree was singing,
angels having joined hands, laughed all around.

BC

The Black Hare
To Nikolai Otsip

The flame of the fir tree goes out, softly in the hall.
In the dark nursery the hero growing tired is sleeping.
And from the ledge with red eyes
motionless the snowy hare looks.

Snow flies from the heavens in a continuous wall,
the streetlamps walk with white caps.
In the field, with a kerosene moon,
the steamer runs on red palms.

The mountains of the wave walk in the ocean.
From the islands the sirens drone threateningly.
And the big ship, wiped out by ice blocks
leaning to one side lies under the starry flag.

There in the cabin the gramophone is playing
and friends are dancing in the half dark.
Losing his balance the dog barks,
the skeleton in a frock coat flies to the ship.

In his hand he has a moon and a rose,
and in the other a letter where there is a yellow curl.
Through the patterns of the starry frost
angels watch after him from the window.

He will not disturb anyone when he comes in.
He will touch the dancers politely with his hands,
and when the night sun rises
the ice will thaw, thaw and the boat sink.

There will only be the starry flag on the white glacier
from the deck in the southern sea.
And the officers take off their service caps.
A short shot flames out in the sea.

The terrible hare with red eyes
behind twin glass, behind layers of cotton wool,
looks slyly: the fir tree goes out in the hall.
The dead bald boy sleeps in his bed.

BC

Homage to Pablo Picasso

The ghost of dawn appeared over the black island.
The loner in the mist whispered the pale blue words,
the horn sang on the bridges with violet motorised barges,
and in the gardens died the blue colour of blossoming hours.

On enormous ropes in the pool is the rusty cruiser
it entreated: 'Let me die in the ocean'.
But the river steamer in smoke and steam, like a geyser,
mocked him and the barges dragged it along with a lasso.

And at the grey tent, in the wagon with yellow wheels
the acrobat and the dancer slept arm in arm on the hay.
Their father, the giant, in a striped sailor's jersey
washed openly on the pure, empty, spring square.

In the morning in the new town pretty children were walking.
The loner watched after them smiling in the mist.
Our circus in flags will be, and the biggest in the world,
it will travel rocking in the green restaurant wagon.

And still they spoke and the stars watched after them,
thus they wanted to play with them, acrobats in the dust.
And the coming years approached dawn's threshold.
And earth's future dawns smiled in sleep.

Only the evening approached. The loner fell asleep from sadness,
and the enormous sunset was a full of a presentiment of eternity.
On the boulevard pretty trumpets in flames began to sound.
And at the grey tent the daubed clown started to sing.

High over the arena on the delicate steel tight-rope
the little girl dancer walked with her tender acrobat.
Suddenly the crowd rose a little and a trumpet sound came abruptly
    to an end
The acrobat and the dancer went into the dawn without return.

High over the houses the airship of sunset was flying,
the bluish evening air went out and became cold.

The blue tsar clouds in radiant tights
rocked serenely on the delicate starry trapezes.

The loner whispered:'Tomorrow again it will be spring on the earth
again it will be the instant to fall asleep at dawn.
Tomorrow eternity is singing: do not forget to die at dawn,
and come from the sunrise to the sunset like heavenly children.'

BC

The Boy and the Angel
To Yuri Felzen

The sun was low, low in the sky
in the black world among black clouds.
The dead rays returned to the hills
in their gold grandeur.

Under the lilac in a muddy lane
a blue-eyed angel was dying,
and over him, returning home from a walk
a tender, drunk boy was guffawing.

What brings you, angelic children,
to cry on the earth among the lilacs?
You should have flown off
on a small wing early at dawn.

I remember, a voice which I'd often heard in dreams
called through the pink twigs:
'It's late, return late, child,
the day is coming from the heavens like blue snow.'

The reflection of the stars freeze in the mirror
over the park—flowers in ice.
The park mirror will be broken with a smile
in spring in hell.

The pink stars of indifference
carry you into the sky on the white day.
Only the angel did not listen to the boy,
he was looking at the lilac falling.

Each little cross, flying past,
sang to him: 'Take me with you'.
Then it melted like snow.
It was the devil who took the boy home to the café.

RM

Pentecost
Boris Zakovich

Dwarfs and gnomes on the cathedral benches
listened to the music with faces like kings.
They sang and prayed in a scarcely audible choir
that the sun would rise from the seas.

Only the night was deep as years
where so many stars had set and will not rise,
the black faces looked at the vaults,
black deacons processed with flowers.

Little sun, sun, we are so tired
of raising small hands to the sky.
The black storms have stopped in the sea,
but still we cannot hear Your roseate voice.

Rise, sun! Our souls will freeze,
we will become big, we'll forget our dream.
A false sun is smiling out of the desert,
the sun is rising from all sides.

They bowed to the ground. The spirits laughed,
hiding their black faces in the columns.
A grey glow appeared in the sky,
the first old nag dragged itself to the slaughter-house.

In the morning when the attendant with the skull-cap
came to sweep the cold cathedral
he was shocked that dead roses
like rubbish were lying on all the benches.

He gathered them up in silence with his waxen hands
and put them in a little coffin in the yard
and went off, getting smaller among the clouds,
to the golden garden, where he lived in summer.

RM

Under the Earth
To Sergei Kuznetsov

The small priest was playing the piano
in a boarded up church, on a snowy night.
The keys quietly sounded and prattled—
they hadn't the power to fight with the snowstorm.

It shook the iconostasis,
extinguished the lamps and cried in the pipes.
The hypostases leaned quietly to the ground
and were swathed in rough, yellow fur-coats.

A vagabond was falling asleep in the deep snow
in a white shirt with a black cross.
He was carrying a present to the church in a small package,
and he fell asleep, under a scraggy bush.

The white hares looked from their holes,
whispered about something, wanted to help.
The wolves scratched at the cathedral doors
but you can't overcome iron with paws.

The dwarfs, angels of the white snowflakes
covered him with their beams,
where the Christmas trees shone with star-candles
asleep in the warmth of their capes.

All was painful in the dense thicket.
The snows' depths and the years ruled everyone,
only the music quietly shone from the Chalice
with the inaudible roseate light of freedom.

The wolves cried. The dead man was gentle,
having fulfilled the covenants of the Holy Grail
and he was only sorry that he had left someone
in the underground chapel at the black piano.

RM

Stars' Poison

In a mysterious theatre vault
they lay on tables—those not of this world.
Professor Moriarty was healing them
from the desire to live and from sadness.

There was a suicide in the class,
he loved to talk about roses with him,
another, afraid of harming himself,
went deep with him into his neuroses.

Nick Carter came there in the morning.
He looked into the eyes of the dead with his magnifying glass.
He reflected: the professor injured them:
he located the addresses of the most proud.

Flying every night into the abyss
with a golden star in his frock-coat pocket,
laughing in sorrow and sympathy
he gave them to drink of the stars' poison.

The blue ones looked into the oceans,
the black ones on the tower called the night.
The white ones descended beyond the mists,
the crimson ones flew away into the sunsets.

But Nick Carter sobbed in the rain:
you see he hadn't worked it out, much as he'd tried,
but the professor suddenly came close,
stealing up to him with his violin.

The poor detective quietly wiped away his tears.
He put the revolver right to his heart.
A metamorphosis came over him:
he left this world as an angel.

RM

Salome I

Softly the angel put out the streetlamps.
One more was extinguished there.
Pegasus galloped above me
blue, white in the dawn's rays.

A strange ghost in the pale light
he moved off and disappeared.
Someone gave a dreadful shout through the window
before the falling of the last stars.

The town was sleeping on big moorings
on the canal, that is empty and small,
far off in the dawning seas
The ship that had gone down was sleeping.

This childhood of mine walked away
in the light blue limitless ocean.
Having dangled her legs in black tights
death flapped on the white mast.

On the stern there was a fine flag
pale scarlet with a gold star,
but high up almost in the clouds
death lay as a black bridal veil.

Salome! Fate rages,
fate flutters disperses the flag.
At your sharp-nosed foot
the star dies in the sand.

The pale blue funny sailor
poisoned himself with the wine of roses,
and his tall ship
passed the pier and set off on a cruise.

It travels along the earth in vain,
all the time tries to shouts and sing.

Death plays in the garden on a trumpet,
the ringing of lilac carries into the alley.

Have mercy, have mercy on him!
Help him to die.

BC

Salome II

The autumn forest turns pink.
On the hills, I am weeping, I am waiting,
Salome, childhood sends you
a star from the heavens.

You are living on a woody slope,
where the flags are grieving on the castle,
dwarfs are dozing in the tall grass,
over the walls swifts are whistling.

The far shore is shrouded in mist,
the sultry evening is burning, burning.
There where the river merges with the sea,
already the unearthly lighthouse reigns.

The pale blue laughing sailor
loads up his steamer
with millions of white roses,
and walks away from the dawn on a cruise.

Salome! Listen, is the steamer
hooting at the earthly lighthouses?
Now it is night in the storm of fate,
he walks away without the sailors.

He will search for his childhood,
he will never find it.
In the ocean, where longing sleeps,
he will be tossed about by the eternal ice.

The storm of fate sounds in the lilacs.
The voice from the sea: I am waiting, I am waiting!'
Salome at the call of the sirens
lifted up the star above the earth.

On the enormous iron tower
all in meditation, he looks into the mist;

throw him into the pale blue abyss,
release the boat into the ocean.

The swimming of the young is irretrievable,
of the pale blue funny hearts.
The waves climb the moonlit stairway
a voice from the sea: 'The end! The end!'

Everything happens in a flash, everything is endless,
the meeting wind, goodbye, goodbye.
The singing of the milky lilacs
the storm of death travels to heaven.

BC

Roses of the Grail
To Olga Nikolayevna Gardenina

Eternity was sleeping in a roseate coffin.
All was quietly strange around.
On the dark blue trumpets the angels
were trumpeting about fate
one early summer, in the emerald sky.

In the dark house a ghost was sleeping on a chair,
leaning on a work table.
The fires of July in the big window
had silently died, slowly sank
shining in the vast depth.

The sunset over Roncesvalles is high,
the evening is motionless, the way is over.
The knights of the Grail beyond the walls
have picked a white rose in the snow
and smiling wait for someone.

The sunset lit the holy vaults.
The kings sleep high in their towers.
Above them in the clear weather
the ships of spring move like years,
the music of the sunset plays off them.

The bell has struck the hours of parting.
Autumn shines high in the mountains.
The sword-bearer will approach
the gates, forget his suffering
and put the rose in his hand, grubby with earth.

He will say quietly that summer has passed.
The gilded globe has turned.
Lord, how everything triumphed!
Only the kings read in the crimson sunset
that Your soul had returned to us.

RM

The Passing

To Sophia Grigorievna Stalinskaya

In the black world, where souls are hostile,
where sunsets call up deaths,
the apple trees quietly in their wedding apparel
go from the suburbs to the fields.

Into the bright yellow smoky sea
it is easier for them to fly away at sunset
than to blossom their last in the roadside dust.
Oh, how children want to die.

Just rarely do the eyes in the sky
open over their halo
and a thunderstorm from heaven
flies down with beautiful, joyful burbling.

In the morning a new arrival goes out
into the damp garden to be a little sad in a hammock.
He sees the apple-tree in white constellations
is dying on the wet sand.

Stepping into the heavy summer
sisters are tenderly jealous of it,
as it goes off into the sunset amidst the dawn
in the pale smoke of the branches.

RM

Pity for Europe
To Marc Slonim

Europe. Europe. With what slow, youthful mourning
your immense flags are stirring in the moonlit air.
Amputees speak laughingly of war,
while the scientist in the park prepares a rocket to the moon.

Bright flags are raised on the tall buildings.
The clock dreams on the tower. Will the experiment be a success?
The sun sinks into the sea with the slow decline
of summer days. The ship disappears in a strip of smoke.

But the soft autumn rain flies onto the lilac road.
The cinema resounds and the teenager buys a ticket.
And in a sky heavy with rain, the mysterious, winged genius
dreams, high up in his skyscraper, of future happiness.

Europe. Europe. Your gardens are full of people.
Ophelia reads a newspaper in a white taxi,
while Hamlet is dreaming of departing to freedom on a tram,
fallen under the wheels with a smile of deathly longing.

The immense sun is setting in the yellow mist.
Far, far off in the suburbs gaslights burst into flame.
Europe. Europe. The boat has sank in the ocean,
as the orchestra in the hall blasts out a prayer on trumpets.

Everyone remembered the trams, the woods and autumn.
Everyone plunged deep in sadness in this pale blue abyss.
Tell me—Are you afraid? Am I afraid? Not really!
I'm a European! laughed the man in evening dress.

I'm English you see. I'm used to the ice in newspapers.
I'm used to submitting, to losing with dignity. And yet,
in London such delicate ladies approach their 'friends',
while shop roses are withering behind thick glass.

The genius on the tower was dreaming of the future:
of glassy blue buildings in the distance, of angel people

flying from the cold earth on the wings of freedom,
heading for the sun where they are free to grieve.

And once more sunsets shone over the roofs of the towers,
where, in love with the sky, they sang of eternal spring.
The following morning people wept from a terrible pity,
having seen the past years by chance in a dream.

Empty boulevards. The soft rain has fallen and become weary,
huddled up against the fence in the cold autumn languor.
There where we died expecting nothing for ourselves—
we, the sick workers of the too tall house:-

under the white stones in the cold yellow dawn,
peaceful as the years, as the drowning duke in evening dress,
like the old professor singing quietly in the dark,
flying off in his iron rocket to the murderous stars.

BC/RM

The Spirit of Music

The clouds were shining above the musical ball,
green burned brightly at the entrance.
There was life, but in ten steps
night shone and the years floated in eternity.
We danced to our life under the noise
of great trumpets, where time rumbled,
the drunk laughed seeing so many moons,
having fallen asleep in the roses and having embraced with decay.
To the challenge of trumpets, over the precipice of the soothsayer,
like the glimmer of rockets wandering in the nights.
They laughed, wept, were sad,
threw roses to the reflection of stars,
they praised secret books,
in the distance they grew silent crossing the bridge.
Everything disappeared, went out, came suddenly to an end,
but the music shouted 'Choir forward!'
Pity rang her hands in the side street
and called people to kill the music
but the angels played serenely.
Grass, flowers and children listened to them,
circling, dancers kissed tenderly
and woke on a different planet.
It seemed to them they were flowering in hell,
and far below was blue air.
The spirit of music dreamed in the night garden
with the enigmatic smile of the nightingale.
There the ball was extinguished there was dawn, peace
only with a slender iron hand
death strummed in requiem,
the sun rose softly over the river.

RM

Angélique

The sun smooths the transparent ice.
The face of the rising winter sleeps.

The sun warms the empty flowers
that grow beyond the wall of darkness.

A tender peaceful world is in the ice.
It sleeps with the pale star at its forehead.

But the young man sees himself
in a dream on another side completely.

On a whale, on a bald moon,
a ghost sees the house of love in glass,

metallic birds in crystal,
a ferry on a green cliff,
Apollo who sleeps in the earth.

But the gramophone sings underground,
a maiden walks on the icebound river,

and a football flies over
the roofs of palaces and dachas.

This world is a violet sparkle.
Terrible roar of stars flying away.

Wild chic of operetta divas.
Returning motif.

The procession of souls passes
under the dreamy street shower,

everyone has sadness and a question,
a negative sense of hell's stench.

Over them in chorus in prison
floating by in the dark is a rank

of surprising, sleeping faces
who have not looked or fallen flat.

But between them is sorcery and rain,
a crazy layer, there is the daughter of hell,

a disgusting, beautiful circus
where there are dancing girls and the dead.

RM

In the Distance

It was quiet in the world, it was late.
A dirty angel forgot his hunger
and lay down to sleep under the starry flag
which was gradually covering the city.

Over the black fan of the health resort room
where the sunset burned the bonfire of sadness,
the sky quietly dissolved the halls.
Ghosts met with night on the towers.

Their voices were serene.
All that was slept before them
on the holy snow white plain.
All that will be—floated scarcely visible.

The stars were woken, eyes were dreamed
on the edge of the heavens, at the frontier of night.
Way below the moon rose.
A night bird wailed.

Time sang from the tower, the tower faded
and the moon stole in wearing only a shirt.
The dirty angel slept in the dawn rays
and a comet sailed to him from the skies.

RM

Winter

To Abram Minchin

A rosy light descends on the white valley,
the sun is rising while the soul sky is appearing.
The angel dances in the rays of the golden mandolin,
In the park of frozen trees the reeds are sparkling.

The winter morning begins with a glow of snow.
Eternity falls silently on the warm hand,
pure eternity descends on the body like tenderness
and disappears falling on the spirit incarnate.

The dead sun dozes on a pink iceberg,
the convict orchestra plays quietly in the dungeon,
black souls have descended with fires to the earth.
The sacred shades of those in love have risen to the heavens.

The snow of the universe falls in the black sky.
A girl of the dawn is wandering among the carriages;
the yellow apparitions of the gaslights sleepily
process quietly their mourning procession after her.

All is going to sleep, the giants on the clock-towers are silent,
everything changes towards the strange morning hours,
the grey sky—a huge whitish cockroach—
crawls to the black heart of the naked dead.

RM

Remember—Resurrect

In a crooked cul-de-sac
a terrifying, black caravan drove by,
the dwarf sun lay crushed
on the stones of an everyday stroll.

We descended under the earth down a ladder,
we searched for the fire at the centre of the earth,
we slithered into silence and dreams
down a huge, black slope.

We descended lower and lower
down infinite crooked corridors.
Then we hear the distant singing
of some strange night conversations.

'Who goes there?' 'Dead memory'.
'Where is love?' 'Returned to the king.'
The snow like a crimson banner covered
the dead who've gone off into the sunset.

They need no fortune, no faith,
absolute night is more dear to them;
those who reached the icy barrier
only want to overcome the year.

Curled up in bed, like children
to deceive the giants of the night,
to go away at dawn to the sunrise world,
to bring back the memory that's gone.

RM

Death Island
To Dina Grigorievna Shraibman

The crimson trumpets sleepily sounded my failure,
the centuries closed on me, the river is covered with snow,
I lie motionless on death island and cry.
The fires of a cloud blossom over me serenely.

The spring is gold and summer strange and long
and there are some white towers where sleepy music breathes
and a comet from the dark sky flies quietly up to them,
but he who plays in the sacred tower does not sleep or hear.

There at a huge height a voice grown hoarse with singing repeats itself.
Everyone is meeting again and laughing at a great distance.
It's as though the abandoned dream of the universe having flown
through the woods sees far away the wintry, sickly sun.

I forgot the names, I fell asleep in the middle of the journey,
the old chestnut tree silently took off its yellow hat over me,
the sun took an age to say farewell and stood in the blue threshold
then went, appearing over the cold as a red moon.

The hoarfrost shines through the grass. As in a future world
distant trumpets ring through the mist at the station.
Long have I seen You asleep in the green ether,
there was a crowd and the stars burned in the resort room.

The mysterious cooling flag floated in the pink sky,
the distanced music poured into the smooth sea,
somewhere in the clear air (it seemed there was an infant crying)
the distant singing of an empty tram was born.

I already realized then that I would have too little eternity
to consider what sort of a mysterious evening it was over the sea,
the people laughed and winced in expectation of snow
and the newspaper vendors shouted about death by the chemist's doorway.

RM

Air Spirit

To Anna Prismanova

Maiden autumn came down from heaven.
Sky blue to the brim.

The white ship of the lonely sinks
quietly in high, bright-eyed seas.

Under the birch tree on the yellow forest
sleeps a handsome forest Jesus.

A gentle hare stands over him
warming his paw on the yellow halo.

Maiden autumn you are beautiful
as my ruined soul.

You are quiet as the dawn mist
in which she went away from the earth.

O Lord God, how easy it is,
how deep, how far from this earth.

She lived in a dark house.
She did no evil to anyone.

She cried a lot, slept a lot.
How good that she died.

If there's no God in heaven,
she'd sleep sweetly in the dark.

Sweeter than lying in gold paradise,
where I'll never come after her.

RM

Lumière astrale

Quieter. Light darkens
secretly in this world.
Smoke crawls and darkness falls,
a breath of snow.
Laughter comes
and kings' death fades.
The gramophone
sings beautiful and clear.
A gentle eaglet soars in the sky
in a golden wreath;
life sleeps in a sack
with a metal pin in the throat.
The ice palace
quietly melts in the sun,
where the pain of hearts
dreams of the future.
Night spirits glower
and are silent,
hell breathes
with flashing fires in the night.

RM

Mystic Rondo III

The cats are cold. They yawn
yes. Yes.
Above the world's tower
butterfly years quietly fly by.

Angels drag bricks
building a white house,
others sleep lazily
in the gold forest.

Maiden autumn has bewitched them
with blueness,
kissed them on their tender childish forehead
by the hill.

Who is walking, singing in the abyss?
Time to sleep.
Two kings are pouring sand
in the blueness.

The day's king is feeble, sickly, tender—
he looks at
how the snow white sand falls
onto the balcony.

He seeks out holy sounds in a book:
the book sleeps.
It has lain down its white pages—
hands on its chest.

The night's king goes to the sun
with a dead head,
he catches butterflies with a slender,
blue net.

Then the time of life flows
like water,

that will always carry Ophelia
to her homeland.

RM

Morella I

The streetlamps faded and night played the piano,
the spectre of dawn appeared already in the bushes.
You silently watched the sunrise with a fixed smile
and it reflected and turned blue on compressed lips.

Morning already appeared over the world like a Medusa mask,
where the dreams of nightingales in the reeds fight with light.
Your mysterious look, accompanying the constellation of the Lyre,
like a falcon, calm, did not see me on the earth.

How you rolled the torn-off pearl with your eagle's claw,
it was as though you were counting my short years.
Why did I lose you? You played like light with the universe,
why did I fall and let the eagle free?

You fluttered like a black eagle in the yellow sunsets,
like a proud, mute eagle you overshadowed fate.
You entered without asking and drew back the tablecloth from the mirror,
and saw eternity, the tender girl, in the coffin.

You, the tender eternity, spread your black feathers,
you fell in love with the shining of your homeland in the yellow sunset.
O, Morella, go to sleep, how terrible are the huge lives,
be like the black kids, forget your motherland, Peri.

Like the mask of Medusa you looked at white time,
the nightingales burnt down, the factories howled in the distance,
only a morning train rushed by beyond the limits,
there where dead eternity in sadness had abandoned the charms of earth.

O, Morella, return, everything sometime will be different,
the light is laughing over us, shut your snow eyes.
Your eaglet is suffering, Morella, crying, crying,
and like mascara, the universe is dissolving in tears.

RM

Morella II

Morella's voice quietly hushed on the other shore,
the moon rushed to the north like a silver falcon,
dead time slept in an open iron coffin,
the snow butterflies quietly sat on the trees around.

A violet sparkle meandered on the snowy steppe.
Like valour of the heavens, in your motionless eyes,
there where the sun was shackled with a terrifying, black chain,
so that it went round in a circle, and an angel stands on the clock.

Sing the valour of Morella, heroes who've gone off to the sea,
this eternity girl has spread the wings of an eagle.
But the snowstorms have burst in and the stars rushed in to the
        cathedrals,
the stars called Morella, not knowing that You have died.

Silently in the moon storm we looked at the sea from the castle,
below the black waves roared out your valour,
the wind ripped from life and poppies howled under the moon,
you, like a black standard flapped at the very edge.

You returned like life, like light flying off into the abyss
you stepped out onto air and quietly went off through the air
and huge snow-stars flew to meet you,
they surrounded you and kissed you endlessly.

Where, oh where are you my brightness? Oh, in what snowy attire
will the trumpet of the Resurrection of the Dead find the two of us?
It's Christmas outside. Tired life sleeps over its fortune telling,
and black-winged fate comes down from the mirror into the world.

RM

Seraphita I

The electric violins appealed out in the darkness,
the ship was sinking to the bottom on the huge screen,
the rain fell noisily on the asphalt. Roulette was rattling in a hut.
Do you remember this spring on the threshold of freedom?

You closed your eyes and went off into the terrible distance,
Tannhäuser in vain shouted about death on the gramophone.
You were far away, perhaps you had ascended to heaven,
the world shone before you like the morning snow and was silent.

Constellations burst and worlds were born in roses,
but I fell by an invisible door in the midst of the song of life.
O Mary, there in the abyss remember my name,
perhaps I'll hear, perhaps I'll remember that shore.

Your dream was so deep that the gilded thread
could break unnoticed. Now you seem not to breathe.
I begged you to go down from the racket of life.
I begged and hoped you wouldn't hear.

But a voice was born. Oh, I didn't understand at first,
it was born in such exhaustion, flew for so long
like a bird that rocked eternity on wings over the sea.
It was surprised with itself and wanted to listen to itself.

'I am with you forever. I don't lose you even in heaven.
I carried away this dark name into the circles of dawn and sunset.
I go to sleep, get lost, get weak, fly, die.
The angel with the white name is with me over the chaos of evil.'

Only light, like a yellow blade, came out of the dark.
The presentation was over. Rainy spring faded.
Time passes quickly, but the heart knows no terror.
The heart hears the praying of names in the circle of the dawn.

RM

Seraphita II

Night moved on. Everything was distinguished for itself,
everything was transformed into something else. It was time for you
       to appear.
We sang in the cave and a girl played cards,
only I came out, was silent and tried to pray.

I returned to the wine. Oh if only you hadn't come!
With all love, generosity, brotherly sadness
would still have done the bidding of the shinings of evil,
because no one knew anything of the dawn.

Everything seemed strange. It was time for you to come down.
There was something in the dawn that did not yet want to wake.
The sun was praying in the abyss, not wanting to rise,
but to cry, to extinguish and to turn into a shroud of rays.

The guitar shouted: 'We deserved better
but they turned away, they forgot us.
Our star-destiny, only in desperate fate, only in dark
and in foul filth can be sensed mad sadness.

Drink black stars! But suddenly the universe flared up.
You came in without asking. We didn't even manage to raise our hands.
We were not expecting you. You came through the abyss to meet us,
we were playing deep underground, we sang out of tune.

You were quiet as the dawn over the factory area,
beautiful as a dusty branch in empty towns.
You stood leaning against the muddy wall like a drunk
and in your eyes there shone tears like birds in the woods.

You looked at the faces, the ash, the discarded cards
and were silent, ready to die a thousand times.
Out of the dark frenzy, in confusion and the smoke of excitement
contemplated the one who was ready to die a thousand times.

The cock crowed, like an angel over the world of shame.
You stretched out your palms and said softly: 'Soon'.

RM

Stoicism

In that warm hour over the darkened world,
the yellow-nosed moon was born,
to be immediately wiped clean with soap:
and at once sensed autumn and the garden.

All day heat had resounded from the tower,
while the people's eyes saw a dream before death . . .
It is late before evening the sorcerer
smiled refreshing with his dark crimson robes.

Under the green twilight of the chestnut trees
the darkish lilac granite was drying out.
The children laughed loudly by the fountain,
drawing the new town with chalk.

In the morning birds were washing themselves
in the aqueduct, while the emperor slept on bare boards.
Already, among the marble and boredom,
a midday hell was breathing from the Euphrates.

But over the castle, beneath a deathly sky,
the immense golden wings stretched out,
and a lifeless victory was smiling
as the soldier lay dozing beneath a layer of dust.

It was stifling. In the wretched bath house
things were stolen, as beggars were shaved;
while in the water we talked of realms,
with a cautious movement of lips.

We spoke of the fine way this world had been silenced,
of how it had been consumed, of how it was evening
in Rome. We spoke of the marvellous, wrongful
death of the broad-shouldered children of wise men.

Glistening athletes were jeering
as the yellow moon flamed up.
But Christ bowed down over Lethe
and listened to us in the awful distance.

The night stars were melting in the sea
and flowers were escaping from the heat.
Indian kings, already awoken, were making
their way over the abyss into Bethlehem.

And the servant of sleeping Pilate
quietly poured water into the cup,
while the centurion on duty cleaned the armour
and Joseph sullenly planed the cross.

BC/RM

The whole day in a cold, dirty shroud ...

The whole day in a cold, dirty shroud
the dreamer slept, forgetting the world.
In the morning there was a swimming contest,
the trumpets played on the tug.

Sweaty rowers shouted from the rowing boats,
the people clapped loudly on the bridges.
In a gust of wind to freedom
the flags tore off the windows and poles.

The wind blew the magazines onto the water,
dust flew from the boulevard into the blue.
By the station a balloon twisted
in the branches of a lime-tree bare of leaves.

All those who hadn't gone away for summer
shuffled the yellow leaves on the boulevard
and squinting at the sky made out
the announcement on the air balloon.

They were all putting on a brave face,
and did not let each other be sad,
as though they had never been wrong,
as though they had expected nothing.

Tired of the motley, lazy day
they returned home exhausted
in the hour when in a sick paralysis
the dreamer rose and opened the window.

RM

The world was dark, cold, transparent . . .

The world was dark, cold, transparent,
long graduating towards winter.
It was close to them who are lonely and depressed,
direct, stern and woken from dreams.

He thought: Calm down, be stern,
all are unhappy, all silent, all waiting,
all wake and laugh and again
doze off, dropping the book on their chest.

Endless nights will soon be here,
lamps will lean low over the tables,
on a steep library bench
the poor man will hide in the corner.

It will become clear that jokingly and secretly
we are still able to forgive God for pain.
Live. Pray behind closed doors.
Read black books in the abyss.

Freezing on empty boulevards
to talk about truth till dawn,
dying blessing the living
and writing without answer till death.

RM

The sun sinks, it's still so hot . . .

The sun sinks, it's still so hot,
autumn is in the air and the park became bare.
There the lemonades burn brightly in the little hut,
and yellow pages of newspapers are in the water.

We're still so young. Rain poured all summer,
but rowing boats rocked beyond the wet glass.
Pistols cracked in the green garden.
How swiftly, how unexpectedly the summer passed.

The blue reflected in the pane so late
and the moon rose over the factory chimney.
The soul of creation—hope for mercy—
perhaps we said farewell to you with the summer.

It's quieter, clearer like this. The prisoner at sunset
is silent in the embrasure of the high prison
and a train on the crooked viaduct whistles
in the bright shining of the autumn azure.

The coaches rock and go west.
The noise of a carousel comes from the boulevard.
He looks at the shining, does not want to cry.
How dusty, how brief is the joy of partings.

Late birds rush over the tower.
How swiftly leaves forget about the sun.
The hand opens the holy pages.
Eyes are closing. Pain recedes.

RM

Supplementary to *Flags* 1927–1930

Dedicated
to
Tatiana Shapiro

Each cold soul burns with dawn's light . . .
To George Ivanov

Each cold soul burns with dawn's light,
empty evenings.
But out on the pavements gaslights are burning
and spring chats with the gardens.
Yesterday there was snow.

The lilac sings beyond the stone walls,
spring is in flame.
And there is a call of sirens in the distance
and racing through the lilac
a car is grieving.

Above the warm river
the gates are wrapped in pink flame.
The village is still asleep,
while the church shines on the hill
so close as if you could touch it with your hand.

Soul, you will roam forever
among the spring snowstorms,
and will wait in the empty suburbs of morning,
while the years fly south
a mass of pink flames.

The nightingale sings there
in the garden, you feel sleepy.
Soul, spring calls to you,
steps laughing onto the thin ice,
falls to the bottom.

The light snow of the lilac has fallen
in the fine hour.
The great angel on the hill,
wearily faded away
in a cold pink flame.

BC

Ancient history is full of blue and pink stars ...

Ancient history is full of blue and pink stars,
of towers from which the dawn is visible,
of butterflies dreamily flying on the bridge.

Morning rises quietly above Rome,
and the shivering soldier walks along.
The polar ice glitters in the sea,
while high above the earth the nightingale sings.

So high, so deep, so far from the earth,
the white boat floats slowly in the mourning sky;
it carries the dead sun—we hear the spectre sing.

'The icy air has warmed up,
and spring has arrived.
Be happy, anyone who dies on earth today,
anyone who will not see in the park how the lilac blooms.'

How penetrating, deep, and far from the earth,
black pipes sing on the bridge, white flags
are raised high as the Roman forces walk.

The butterflies fly quietly above them,
and above every iron halo.
The sun rises quietly above the statues:
new days will come.

'Praise to him, who doesn't wait for the spring,
to the rose who doesn't want to live', the snake-nightingale
dressed in the moon, whistles in the pink park.

'Sleep and wait, child tsars,
midnight, leave us, morning return.
Everything will be just like we dreamed in the sea.
Everything will be just like we asked in grief.'

Eternity sings at dawn,
Nazareth keeps silent in the roses.

BC

My moon I can dream about you again . . .
To Tatiana Shapiro

My moon I can dream about you again.
Spring will pass.
The bird goes back to the sun in a dream,
the ice has broken up.

Above the white houses the dream of spring seas,
the light of clouds,
and the tender glimmer of the bright green canopy,
flames of the ages.

The children's swift flight to meet the snow,
their terrible height,
the fall of roses into the shining river,
the gliding of the stars.

The glimmer of the nightingale in the dark lilac night,
the sound of hands.
The river opens wide its blue eyes,
dawn is all around.

And the scarlet wind above the empty fence,
love, love.
And the sudden shot of the waking mountain,
the birth of words.

The falling of the white house into the gorge,
the ebb of war.
In the cafe the playing of the hollow cello
beneath the rays of the moon.

See how quickly the frost's blue lights
crawl past.
The night skeleton sneaks on tiptoes
into our dreams.

And like a deer along the snow of the milky tundra
love runs
but all the same eternity shines on the bottom of the river,
and there is blood in our veins.

Although a hundred deaths threatened the sacred animal,
the sacred spring,
and with an air of importance the sleeping executioner
walks beyond the glass door.

Although in the dark the battle-axe
leans towards my hands
and the great shadow of the earth
lies on the ceiling.

BC

The pale blue soul of the ray ...

The pale blue soul of the ray
taught me to be silent.
I hear the dreamy singing of the stream,
my little garden sleeps, whispering in the rays.

I fell silent I walked on to the sand
I lay on the grass like a mild ox,
above me the jasmine blossomed,
a golden assumption of bees.

I am at peace, I am sleeping in the ages,
the ghost of a thought, that was in flight,
day and night it lies at my feet,
I stroke my enemy.

I am subdued, I am empty, I am simple.
I push away the stars, rays,
above me roses are swaying,
and there is the distant singing of thunder.

Everything has gone, everything has returned again,
I am sleeping in sacredness, in the gold in the emptiness.
Oh God! Bring love
over my jasmine bushes.

Let me be saved from the flames,
let my angel fall asleep in tears.
Everything forgave for the childhood of days
I have my whole life ahead of me.

The boy is looking, the white boat . . .

The boy is looking, the white boat
sails away along the horizon,
in spite of the clear weather,
opening the black umbrella of smoke.

The boy is thinking: but I remained,
I shall never see far off countries again.
Why did the captain never think
to take me with him to sea?

The boy is weeping. The sun looks from a height
and is clearly visible to the sun.
On the boat the pale blue rats
brought the plague from Africa.

The sailors were dying in the white mortuary,
the steam fell asleep in the steel box,
and the little steamer collided in the sea
with the icy blue wall.

But on the tower the angel is meditating,
motionless white in the wicker chair.
He knows, the captain from England
will never return to his bride.

That having abandoned our summer for ever,
the boats moved away in the peace of sunset,
where athletes were sad missing the North,
sailors in striped sweaters.

The ship's boy smiling hauls his fate,
the same as you or me, my friend.
Captain where are the Hesperides?—in the sky
north once more, then further to the south.

Music sings in the white hall.
Wearing a star on your hat, you walked

into the restaurant, my friend, to do nothing and be sad
about the last of the distant countries.

Where the dying steamer fell asleep
and to where the river carries the flowers.
And my soul, laughing, walks away
along the sand in a sailor's suit.

BC

Autumn walks beyond the walls of life . . .

Autumn walks beyond the walls of life
and sings with closed eyes.
Blind bees visit the garden.
Summers fails its exams.

Everything passes smiling kindly.
It is easy and frightening to stay in life.
Autumn wrings its hands in the sky
and sings in the gilded tower.

Chimneys reflect in the evening hour.
The stars rise, the years set out,
and the holy monk rings for vespers.
The sounds of the bell ringing are flying slowly into the mountains.

Life rests in autumn worlds.
In the blue of the sea, in the zenith of heaven
she sleeps under the warm coniferous
at the foot of the granite castle.

And above them in the golden emptiness
the blue path seems endless.
Silently the golden leaves are flying silently
to the stone angel on the breast.

BC

The supernatural knight on a horse ...
To Paul Fort

The supernatural knight on a horse
passes in complete silence,
over the enchanted sword,
about what, about what is he thinking?

The hermit sleeps in the desolate hole
the tree sleeps in its bark,
the moon sleeps on a flat roof,
the magician puffs in a sweet dream.

Motionless boats on the pond,
the hermit sleeps, the sands have become hot.
Merlin passes along the water,
without having stirred the nocturnal flowers.

Merlin, sweetest Jesus,
meets nine muses in the forest.
Madonnas, nine tender maidens,
reverberate with him in the water.

He begins to sing softly,
adders listen in the grass.
Silver fish float to the net
submitting to fate.

Nocturnal Orpheus, saviour of sleep
can scarcely be heard singing in the reeds.
His waning moon
shines slowly in the soul.

Cursed world, you are close to me,
I was born there, where in the darkness
the mermaid hears the singing
having swept back her hair from her face.

But in the dark blue crystal
the cockerel sang, still asleep
Merlin-Hermit rose from his knees,
morning began on the earth.

BC

The air is dark. In the sky roses are soaring . . .

The air is dark. In the sky roses are soaring.
Soon it is the time for streetlamps.
Gently the sultry town turns to evening.
Slowly it becomes dark.

The yellow smoke under the low moon
the late hour, the inexplicable light.
My God! How heavenly is spring
and it's impossible to sleep and there is no happiness.

Clearly audible, how the wheel of fortune
cracks in the temporary military hut in the gas light.
The smell of leaves. A voice in the darkness,
and in the window the stars all burn at once.

My God! Why have they returned again
these leaves in the sky of bright days,
this brightness of dresses, noise of the streets,
evening—a chaos of happiness and lights.

Exhibitions at the town gates,
in the wind advertisements over the bridges
and in the dust, exhausted, weary
the glance of people, who have returned with flowers.

In the evening in the spring glow,
the granite of the roadway becomes more lilac.
The town is calm and empty on Sunday,
in the evening the nightingale shines.

In the late hour among the starry boulevards
do not search, do not weep, do not speak,
listen to the marvellous useless voice
force yourself down towards the terrible dark truth!

The world is terrible. The sun smells of death.
Pride destroys and the lilac chokes with its odours.

Pity everyone, believe no one.
Sweetly destroy your souls!

Laugh, weep, kiss the sick hands,
turn into stone, lie, steal.
Everything is only like the parting of nightingales,
and for everyone ruin is ahead.

Everything here is only scarlet weariness,
a dark dream of lilac on the water.
In the blue sky there is only dust and pity,
the terrible glamour of the unearthly snow-storm.

BC

Night revolved around the trumpet of the orchestra ...

Night revolved around the trumpet of the orchestra,
the last hour sank on the shallow place.
I embraced you with the hand of Orestes
the last time we danced together.

The last time the trumpets rallied the soldiers at dawn.
Dancing we dreamed of destruction
but the public hall turned pink above the flat sea,
in the pine-filled park the birds twittered.

The window burned on the tall dacha,
the orangish sand squeaked with the damp.
The soul slept, used to failure,
already another pink world was flying above.

It seemed to her that the roses were dreaming of something.
They whispered to me having closed their eyes.
Dandies said goodbye, the pale blue faces,
debauched maidens looked to the heavens.

Illuminated with future ages
you walked with them as Abel walked to the sacrifice.
In the distance you merged with the clouds
and I walked onto the funeral boat.

BC

Bibliography

Adamovich, G. *Odinochestvo and svoboda*. Moskva: Respublika. 1996.
Allain, Louis and Olga.Griz. *V Otsenkax i Vospominaniayax Sovremennikov*. St Petersburg: Logos. 1993.
Berberova, Nina. *The Italics are Mine*. Trans. Ph Radley. New York: Alfred Knopf. 1992.
Burchard, Amory. *Klub der Russischen Dichter in Berlin 1920–1941*. München: Verlag Otto Sagner in Kommission. 2001.
Carlisle, Olga. *Poets on Street Corners: Portraits of Fifteen Russian poets*. New York: Random House. 1968.
Karlinsky, Simon and Alfred Appel, Jr. *The Bitter Air of Exile: Russian Writers in the West 1922–1972*. Berkeley: University of California Press. 1977.
Lautréamont, Comte de. *Maldoror and Other Poems*. Trans. Paul Knight. Harmondsworth: Penguin, 1978.
Livak, Leonid. *How it was Done in Paris: Russian Émigré Literature and French Modernism*. Madison: Winconsin Univ. Press. 2003.
_____. 'The Place of Suicide in the French Avant-Garde of the inter war period' in *The Romanic Review* 91 no 3 (2000) 245–62.
McKane, Richard. Ed. *Ten Russian Poets: Surviving the Twentieth Century*. London: Anvil Press Poetry. 2003.
Menegaldo, Hélène. *Poeticheskaya Vselennaya Borisa Poplavskovo*. St Petersburg: Aleteia. 2007.
Ponomareff, Constantin. V. 'Boris Poplavsky: a Poet of Unknown Destination' in *One Less Hope: Essays on Twentieth Century Russian Poets*. New York: Rodopi. 2006.
Poplavsky, Boris. *Sobranie sochinenii*. 3 vols. Berkeley, California: Berkeley Slavic Specialities, 1980-81.
_____. *Sochineniia*. St Petersburg: Letni Sad. 1999
_____. *Stikhotvoreniya*. Tomsk: Vodoleya. 1997.
_____. *Proza vol II: Apollon Bezobrazov i Domoy s Nebes*. Noscow: Soglasie. 2000.
_____. *Avtomaticheskie stikhi*. Moscow: Soglasie. 1999.
_____. *Neizdannoe*. Moscow: Khristianskoe izdatel'stvo. 1996.
_____. *Pokushenie s negodnymi sredstvami* Moscow: Gileia-Goluboi vsadnik. 1997.
_____. 'Dnevnik T.' *Novy zhurnal* 195 (1994): 175–211.

Raeff, Marc. *Russia Abroad: A Cultural History of the Russian Emigration 1919–1939*. Oxford: 1990

Schlögel, Karl. *Das Russische Berlin: Ostbahnhof Europas*. München Pantheon. 2007.

Struve, Gleb. *Soviet Russian Literature*. London: George Routledge and Sons Ltd, 1935.

_____. *Russkaya literatura v izgnanii* New York, 1956; 3rd edn. Moscow: Russki put' 1996.

Struve, Nikita. *Soixante-dix ans d'émigration russe: 1919–1989*. Paris. 1996.

Urban, Thomas. *Russische Schriftsteller im Berlin der zwanziger Jahre*. Berlin: Nicolaische Verlagsbuchhandlung GmbH., 2003.

Varshavski, Vladimir. *Nezamechennoe Pokolenie* New York: Izdatel'stvo imeni Chekhova. 1956.

Williams, Robert C. *Culture in Exile: Russian Émigrés in Germany: 1881–1941*. Ithaca and London: Cornell Univ. Press, 1972.

Zimmer, Dieter. *Nabokovs Berlin*. Nicolai, 2001.

www.ingramcontent.com/pod-product-compliance
Lightning Source LLC
Chambersburg PA
CBHW031155160426
43193CB00008B/380